BLOOM, NOT GLOOM

Self-awareness Explored

Ann-Marie McMahon is a graduate of University College Dublin and a registered psychologist. She is Director of After-care at St John of God Hospital, Stillorgan, County Dublin, where her particular interests include counselling and psychotherapy.

She has a degree in Economics and Public Relations, and has worked in these related areas, as well as in personnel management.

She conducts courses in Personal Development, Human Relations and Communications for the Community and Adult Education Centre at St Patrick's College in Maynooth.

She is presently completing her Ph.D in Human Relations at Pacific Western University, LA, USA.

Ann-Marie's first book is entitled *Issues, not Tissues: A fresh approach to personal development*.

Sylvia Thompson has an honours degree in pyschology from Trinity College Dublin and is presently working as a freelance journalist.

Bloom, not Gloom!

Self-awareness Explored

Ann-Marie McMahon

with

Sylvia Thompson

Illustrations by

Alan Corsini

BROOKSIDE

This book was typeset by
Gilbert Gough Typesetting, Dublin for
Brookside Publishing, 2 Brookside, Dundrum, Dublin 14.

© 1995 Ann-Marie McMahon

Editor: Carole Devaney

Illustrations: Alan Corsini

A catalogue record for this book is
available from the British Library.

ISBN 1-873748-01-9

Printed in Ireland by
Betaprint Ltd, Dublin

CONTENTS

DEDICATION

To all those suffering in silence

ACKNOWLEDGEMENTS

Firstly, I would like to thank Sylvia Thompson who assisted me in writing this book. Her journalistic skills and sense of professionalism made it all possible. Thank you, Sylvia, for all your support and enthusiasm throughout this project.

Alan Corsini enlivens the book with his wonderful illustrations. Thank you, Alan — your contribution has helped the book to bloom.

Carole Devaney, Editor par excellence, rounded it all off with her computer skills and creative flair for writing. Thank you, Carole — our time was short but we had good fun.

I would especially like to thank Gerard O'Connor who risked a second book with me! Thanks too to my publishers — Edwin Higel and his team at Brookside Publishing.

Finally, a special 'thank you' to all the people who have drifted through my life and inspired me to write *Bloom, not Gloom!*

PREFACE

Gloom — what does it mean? At various times, it is a word that enters our minds, but sometimes the meaning does not convey what is really happening in our lives. Unfortunately, life is not a bed of roses for us all. In fact, sometimes we experience life as a garden of weeds, neglected, deserted, desolate.

The weeds represent the chaos in our lives. Fear, anxiety, pain, loneliness, sadness — these are some of the components of our unruly gardens. There are days when the only energy we have is to look at the shambles and ponder on its ugliness. Sometimes, we don't even know how this 'ugliness' developed. Flowers bloom, seasons change, and yet the ugliness remains. How often do we wish that we were those flowers that can change with the seasons, are cared for, watered and nourished to bloom again.

Bloom, not Gloom! will help you to create a garden within yourself. It will help you to throw out those weeds, nourish your emotional self, widen your horizons and free yourself from any invisible pain.

So now is the time to spring into action and create that change you've always wanted!

CHAPTER 1

LIGHTEN YOUR LOAD:

Removing negative baggage

Do you ever feel *really* 'cheesed off'? Sometimes or a lot of the time? Maybe with individual aspects of your life, such as your job or your hobbies or your home or your circle of friends? Or maybe sometimes all of these things combine to make you feel 'stale'? You think your life is stagnant or going nowhere except around in circles, and you keep repeating the same old mistakes every time.

Do you ever feel you deserve better, that life in a way has dealt you a hard blow and that everyone around you seems to be having a better time than you? You wonder if your life will ever change.

The worst part of it may be that you think you have no one to talk to, no one to share your feelings with. Perhaps you don't even know what you would say if you had a 'good listener'. So you go on suffering in silence, believing that many other people also live their lives like this and that maybe this is what life is all about. Some days, you may feel so paralysed by fear and loneliness that even if you saw a way out, you couldn't take it.

You are probably constantly telling yourself things like 'no one thinks or feels like me', 'I'm all alone and no one understands how bad my life is'. Although you may be surrounded by a family or sharing an apartment with friends, you still feel alone. Even when other people try to convince you to change something in your life, reminding you that negativity and self-doubt don't help, you ignore their advice even though you know they're probably right.

If you feel, or have ever felt, any of these emotions, then read on! You may not identify with all of the situations described in the following pages, but you'll probably recognise some of them. Being aware of a problem is the first step to solving it and it is hoped that this book will motivate you to feel a lot better about yourself quickly and painlessly.

FEELING STUCK

Perhaps you really do feel stuck, locked into a certain way of life. You have probably tried to get out or become unstuck. But the old way of living is so familiar to you that you would nearly feel naked if you left it behind.

In some ways, you want to change your life, but you know this would bring its own responsibilities. You avoid responsibility and in so doing lose out on freedom. Sometimes, you want to change your mind, but your fear is so strong and your feelings so rigid that flexibility is impossible for you.

You want help. You know it will strengthen you, but you think you will be perceived as weak. Okay, admit it — you are full of guilt, pain, conflict and self-criticism. You want to get rid of these negative feelings, but you are holding onto them tightly. The big question is why?

Your vocabulary is full of statements like 'I should . . .', 'I must . . .', 'I have to . . .' Your way of behaving never changes and you simply come up with excuses if somebody challenges you in any way. You know well that to change means to take risks and this is something you find extremely difficult to do.

FACING REALITY

In a strange way, you've managed to survive. Perhaps fantasy has been your world of comfort and helped you to avoid the pain of reality. Reality can hurt and it is this pain that prevents you from making any changes. Unlike a stomach ache, emotional pain cannot be seen. You find it difficult to talk about it.

There are times when you would really like to expose your feelings, to tell somebody about your fears, your anger, your guilt. But you believe that it is not acceptable in society to talk about these things and you probably feel that no one would listen or understand you anyway.

So what do you do? You end up bottling it all up inside. You bury your feelings deeper or perhaps you go around wearing a mask so that you portray one image and feel something completely different. Without really knowing it you are, in fact, making life more difficult for yourself.

You want to move forward, but you feel you don't know how. You don't even know what the first step is. You can't articulate it. All you know is that you don't feel right about yourself.

SUPPORT

Some days, you wish you had something more dramatic happening in your life so that you could get some support. For example, if someone had died you could talk about it, you could unburden your problems to people and they would listen. They would empathise with you and perhaps you could also unload some other burdens you've been carrying around for a long time.

For many of us, there are times when nothing dramatic has happened, but we are just not feeling content. Some of us are relieved when we discover that maybe we have a 'flu coming on because then at least we can go to the doctor, who will listen for the ten minutes or so we are there. But we know that this is not enough. You come away feeling listened to, but not really understood. Perhaps you were afraid to tell the doctor what was actually going on.

This book will help you to feel listened to and understood, to feel there is support and help no matter how complex or simple your situation. Everyone has some sort of issue. The aim throughout this book is to help you to come to terms with any discomfort in your life and help you to change yourself in such a way that you feel comfortable to be with yourself no matter what the situation.

THE WAY FORWARD

- Well done — you've got this book and survived Chapter 1! You are on the right road. Decide now to complete it.

- En route, make notes of situations or events that make you feel uncomfortable.

- Decide now to make changes, to give yourself what you really want.

- Welcome to the club! There are millions like you today — feeling a little fragile.

CHAPTER 2

EMOTIONAL NUTRITION:

Needs, not weeds

We all like to feel needed. It gives us a lovely warm, glowing feeling of being secure, protected and wanted. There is no doubt that this feeling is good for us. However, some of us grow up without it; we can feel that nobody loves or cares about us, almost to the extent that we don't care about ourselves.

You may ask why this happens? Sometimes there isn't an obvious reason like, for example, you were orphaned or adopted, or you were number eight in your family. Often, there is no obvious reason at all — you could be an only child and still not feel needed. In many ways, you may have thought you had the perfect parents, but maybe their striving for perfecton actually left you feeling unwanted.

NOURISHING NEEDS

The struggle to be needed can end up in a life full of weeds, not needs. When we look at a garden full of weeds, what do we see? We see chaos. We see an undernourished, uncared-for space. We see a wilderness with no design or pattern. There is a sense of desertion, of neglect. Unlike a garden that is well cared for, a garden of weeds is neglected and will remain so unless somebody makes a decision to start looking after it again.

Sometimes people don't believe they have needs. They go around feeling that they don't deserve anything. This feeling comes from being told as a child that you have to be grateful for everything you get or that you don't deserve anything just for being yourself. You may have been brought up in a very rigid structure where everything you did was monitored and you could never express your feelings. And even if you did, nobody would listen to you anyway.

Feelings are nestling inside us from the moment of birth. A child cries because it needs food. We hear the cry, we see the anxious look and we give the baby food — the crying stops, the child smiles. Most people find it easy to deal with what they see or touch, but it is very difficult to deal with what we can't see — our emotions.

Some people are brought up in an environment where they have no permission to discuss what is going on for them inside. Boys, for example, are often told not to cry, so they learn to bury their emotions. If you never learn to deal with your emotions, you can go around not knowing what is going on inside you, expressing anger in inappropriate situations and contexts. You grow up wondering why you don't get on with people.

GROWING UP

Children growing up in an atmosphere where needs are not heard or met can resort to extreme behaviour which can leave them isolated. They can become stuck in a type of behaviour that is not acceptable to others, but for them is the only way they can communicate their feelings.

There is no doubt that we need to learn to educate ourselves about what is going on inside us and to nourish it in such a way that we don't have to be suffering to the extent that we do.

We all have different needs at different times in our lives. When we are young, we need to be cared for and protected. As we grow older, our needs change. We have a need to learn and to acquire knowledge. As teenagers, we have a need to separate ourselves from our parents and explore new areas. Then, in our twenties, we have a need to define ourselves in terms of our job or our status. Later, some of us have a need to reproduce and start a family. As we get older, our roles reverse and we can again feel the need to be cared for and protected.

There is no perfect time for any need to be met. But what we have to recognise is that we do have certain needs and that we have a right for these needs to be met. In other words, we need emotional nutrition. If we don't get it, our needs become weeds.

Some people live their lives fulfilling everybody else's needs, never their own. Often, they don't know what their own needs are. Such people can become miserable as time goes on because they never get to find out what it is that makes them happy and content.

Other people fall into the 'poor me' syndrome. They are constantly looking on at others, thinking they have it all, believing that everything is alright for them when in fact their expectations could be entirely different. The secret is to avoid comparing your insides with someone else's outsides. Your needs are your own. Learn to recognise them, label them and nourish them.

Think of the garden of weeds again and ask yourself — Do you want this? Or would you rather have a healthy garden, full of your favourite flowers and trees, watered and nourished, peaceful and relaxed.

EMOTIONAL NUTRITION

There is no doubt we need emotional nutrition just as much as we need food for our bodies and knowledge for our brains. It is never too late and unlike the rest of our bodies, we can pride ourselves that our feelings don't age — like a good wine, they mature. We learn from a young age to nourish ourselves so that we grow strong and healthy. We learn to develop our minds through learning and we are taught what we require for success or future development. However, no one ever teaches us that we need to recognise, develop and nourish our emotions too.

Some of us live in such a way that we don't express our emotions, but we dump them onto other people by blaming them and wanting them to take responsibility for us. This may leave us free from responsibility, but in another way, it leaves us confused and dependent on others for everything we feel.

Let's take an example. John and Mary attend a social event together. While Mary thoroughly enjoys herself, John feels ill at ease and even more so because he sees Mary chatting away freely to all their friends and being introduced to new people. On their return home, John tries to blame Mary for his uncomfortable feelings by saying that she ignored him all evening.

FACING A CRISIS

Emotional well-being is an area that is sadly neglected. It is often only when we move into adulthood or we are faced with a crisis that we really begin to understand our true emotions. Sometimes it takes counselling or therapy for people to realise they have all these feelings inside that have never been cared for, expressed, heard, labelled or even listened to.

In such cases, the emotions of the present and those of the past all come gushing forth. We suddenly realise that there are other emotions which have been hidden for the last 30 or 40 years and in the passing of time have become all mixed up. They've piled up, one on top of the other. Sometimes this feels heavy and the feelings are unwelcome. This is because you may still have to deal with certain emotions that should have been dealt with as a child and this is a difficult process. In fact, some adults are children in older bodies.

When we learn to deal with our emotions, we can also learn to understand our needs better because we get to know what it is we need to make us feel comfortable. In many ways, as a result of the emotional nutrition, we become more assertive, less aggressive or passive depending on the situation.

The bottom line is that you have to discover what your needs are and in so doing learn to fulfil them yourself, instead of spending your life wanting other people to meet your needs. So throw out the weeds — and start to enjoy life.

THE WAY FORWARD

- Make friends with your needs. Admit that you have certain needs in your life, be it love from your family, loyalty from your friends, acknowledgement for things you've done well.

- Nourish your emotional system by acknowledging what situations make you happy, sad, angry, guilty and all those other feelings.

- Deal with your negative emotions by admitting them, changing your focus where possible or accepting them where necessary.

- Enjoy your positive emotions to the full and find ways and means of helping them to grow.

CHAPTER 3

HOW ARE THINGS?

The power of language

When you meet somebody unexpectedly, whom you haven't seen for a time, you usually ask 'How are things?' You don't even stop to listen when the other person replies casually, 'Oh, fine'. You pass on without really considering what the reply meant because 'how are things' is such a common expression that it has become meaningless.

Many of us use these words when we simply want to nod to somebody and we don't ever leave time for the person to respond. Perhaps that friend who answered 'Oh, fine' was feeling pretty down and would have welcomed your company over a coffee. However, you were so wrapped up in your own world that you just strolled by and never really waited for a reply.

ACKNOWLEDGEMENT

Some of us live our lives constantly meeting people, but never really acknowledging them or taking on board how they really are. In such cases, people are merely a means to an end. Sadly, we are often so caught up in moving in 'the fast lane' and gaining material success that people become objects in our quest for better things.

You might even consider yourself a good communicator at social events or a good public speaker. But while you appear to communicate well, the reality is you talk *at* people, not *with* people. You never put into practice the golden rule of good communications — listening.

LISTENING

Listening is perhaps the most difficult part of communicating. Many people live their lives never really listening — either to others or to themselves. We not only need to listen to the words; we also need to listen to what is behind the words and particularly to what is not being said.

Body language is also a subtle way of conveying disinterest in a conversation. If you look bored or position yourself away from the direction of the person who is speaking, they can often pick this up as a negative reaction to what they are saying, without either person even acknowledging the body language.

Sometimes in a conversation, silence can say more than words. In an intimate relationship, silence can be a very powerful weapon. It can be used to demean or punish someone. By not saying something, you are cutting off the other person and diminishing them in whatever way you can. However, regardless of how powerful this gesture feels, you are not confronting the issue by remaining silent and therefore not working it out for yourself either.

This sort of behaviour is most common in one-to-one relationships or between parents and their children. Parents who respond to their children with silences are reacting in a very negative and immature way. The underlying message given to the children is that the adults are afraid of whatever it is they won't discuss and this can leave the children feeling insecure in later life. Alternatively, it can make children feel confused because they didn't quite understand the reason behind such an intense reaction.

WORDS

Language is a very powerful form of communication. The words we use can be very emotive. They can control and shape our inner voice. When we are angry, we tend to use words that will shock someone else. But what we are really trying to do is to express our inner turmoil to see if the person on the receiving end will support our anger. However, instead of supporting our anger, generally what happens is that the other person retreats back into themselves and feels hurt by the anger.

VERBAL ABUSE

We often talk about our abhorrence for physical violence, but we rarely consider how a person can be violent in their use of language. You can actually hurt somebody by accusing them in the wrong, attacking them in an aggressive manner or by verbally abusing them.

It is perhaps a more subtle form of violence. Once words are thrown out, they cannot be taken back. The receiver stings almost as if he were being hit, although he can't touch or feel the sting in the same way as he would a weapon. Violence may seem an over-dramatic word to use, but verbal abuse or verbal violence is as painful as any other form of assault.

Individuals who constantly use strong, inappropriate language are, in many ways, getting rid of aggression inside themselves but at the expense of others. It is not very pleasant to sit and listen to people who use offensive language, but these people consider it almost their right because they are sometimes letting off aggressive feelings.

AVOIDING TACTICS

Other people can use silence or act in a very passive way which can be manipulative. Instead of getting rid of their negative feelings, they keep them inside and make others feel uncomfortable by their lack of 'approval' in a conversation.

In the same way, people use sarcasm as a means of ridding themselves of their negative feelings. Making a sarcastic comment can easily offend and can make the other person feel really bad; it may temporarily relieve you of your own negativity, but it doesn't deal with it properly.

In many ways, language is a method of revealing what goes on inside. When we hurt, it is much easier to hurt someone else than to experience the pain ourselves and accept it. This is why many people go down the road of 'blame talk'. Blaming somebody else, particularly via the use of language (in other words, you tell half a dozen other people what has happened), takes all the limelight off yourself and focuses the attention on other people. It is a very clever form of not taking responsibility for what you do or of confronting the situation for yourself if appropriate.

Sometimes people are very good at making excuses when they don't want to accept responsibility for what they've done. Again, excuses are made through the use of language. When we make excuses, we shift responsibility from ourselves onto something or someone else, thereby avoiding having to look at what is going on for ourselves. Another shifting technique is denying — when you say you know nothing about something when the reality is you know all about it but don't want to accept it.

INTERPRETATION

The other important issue in language is the interpretation of words. How we interpret something determines how we respond to it and how we feel at that particular moment influences how we will interpret what is being said. For example, if you are feeling good about yourself and somebody makes a joke about one of your negative characteristics, say your height, you will probably laugh it off and think no more about it. But if you are feeling low in yourself and not very confident, such a comment can be devastating to your self-esteem.

Learning to interpret appropriately what is being said to you goes back to feeling more confident yourself. If you feel good about yourself, you won't worry too much about someone who blames you in the wrong (because you know it is not true) or someone who speaks aggressively to you or even someone who glares at you in silence instead of dealing with the issue at hand.

THE WAY FORWARD

- Stop, look and listen — you can only change your vocabulary and the way you use words if you first become aware of them. Listen out for negativity, aggressiveness, sarcasm and silences in your own speech patterns.

- Look at the way people react to you — do they take you seriously? too seriously? or seriously enough? Are you getting across the message you want to get across?

- Listen to what is being said to you, how it is being said and what is not being said.

- Learn that every conversation is a two-way process, not just one person 'sounding off' without being aware of the effect it will have on the other.

CHAPTER 4

FACING FEAR:
The great intimidator

Most of us will admit to feeling frightened about something at some stage in our lives. We generally conquer these fears as we get older, although sometimes we replace earlier fears with new and more painful ones.

Do you remember as a child being afraid of the dark after someone told you about the 'bogey man'. As a child you didn't have the words to question this idea, but you knew you were afraid. Some children are lucky in that their parents sit down and comfort them from such fears, making them feel secure and safe. Other children aren't so fortunate and grow up with a fear of being alone, abandoned or perhaps even rejected.

This fear of being alone can stay with you for a long time and can prevent you from separating yourself from others. For example, some people find it very difficult to leave home for the first time. Others may end up entering a relationship that isn't ideal rather than be on their own. The fear of being alone can stay with you even when you are in a relationship, although you may only realise this when things turn sour with your partner. A fear of being alone can, in fact, prevent you from getting to know your own needs, desires, emotions and frustrations.

REJECTION

When we are rooted in fear, we sometimes don't realise what is really going on inside us. Feelings of abandonment, rejection and shame can leave us behaving in very passive ways. For example, people who label themselves as shy or lacking in confidence or introverted may, in fact, be projecting themselves this way due to a deep-seated sense of fear that they may not recognise or cannot articulate. All they know is that they are uncomfortable and unable to cope in certain situations.

Let's take, for example, Mary. As a child, she had a very strong fear of being left alone because she feared somebody would 'take her away'. When Mary was seven years old, she spent some time in hospital and this reinforced her fear of being abandoned. While she only spent a month there, to Mary it was a life-long sentence.

Although she came home quite happy, the feeling of being abandoned never left Mary. At 24, she met John and got married, and it seemed as if they would live 'happily ever after'. However, John had to go away on business for a time, leaving Mary alone. Suddenly, Mary felt she couldn't cope. John was not aware of her fears. While he was away, she telephoned him to say that she wasn't sleeping properly; she had to go to the doctor to get something to relax. She felt her world was caving in. John couldn't understand this since up to now they had had a very happy relationship.

When John came home, Mary relaxed. But he was always aware that there was pressure on him not to go away again on business. It wasn't until Mary eventually went into therapy that she discovered the source of her fear. When she finally expressed it, she was able to deal with it and, fortunately, they solved what could have turned out to be a continuing problem in their marriage.

COMMITMENT

Unlike the example of Mary and John above, some people grow up with a fear of committing themselves to an intimate situation. Their fear is not of being alone, but of being in a relationship. It is in some ways similar to Mary's fear in that it is rooted in a fear of being rejected. They play safe, sit on the fence, hoping that nobody will ever find them out, but they live in constant inner pain and turmoil. These people often have great barriers built around them. They seem able to organise their lives well, and they appear confident in their work and social activities.

Often the source of such a fear lies in early family experience. If, for example, as a child you noticed that your parents fought and argued a lot and issues never got resolved — somewhere in your mind, you may have decided that you certainly didn't want a relationship like theirs. In later life, you realise that all relationships have this potential, so you feel that only by avoiding such involvement altogether can you protect yourself from being hurt.

MARGINALIZED

Some fears can relate to how society perceives us. If you are seen as being in any way different to 'the norm', either physically, mentally or emotionally, you can become marginalized by society and treated as an 'outsider'. This threat of feeling rejected can create havoc in your life. And in addition, you have all the other daily fears to deal with, such as fear of the unknown, fear of the future or fear of what might go wrong. The net result of all this emotional trauma means that you need plenty of support to cushion yourself.

RESPONSIBILITY

Sometimes people feel so afraid of what is going on in their lives that words fail them. They cannot express or articulate what is going on, but inside their being is screaming out for someone to listen to them or at least to ask the right question.

This sort of fear can make you feel so bad that you can't get up in the morning. For example, Johnny decided to buy a new house, which for most people is a fairly natural progression in life. However, Johnny felt terrified by the enormity of his decision. He was scared by the responsibility of owning a house and of having to pay for it for the rest of his life. Sometimes even someone in the throes of getting married feels frightened, but is afraid to say so.

CHANGE

Fear can, in some cases, actually prevent us from taking opportunities when they present themselves. We often postpone enjoyment by holding on to our fears. Fear of the unknown and fear of the future are two of our worst enemies. Even when somebody tells you that doing something will turn out to be to your advantage, you still won't do it. You feel rooted, paralysed. To others, you seem stubborn, awkward and even hostile, because they don't understand the extent of your fear.

Fear prevents us from changing. It gets us stuck in such a way that we often end up as our own worst enemies. We often hear people say things like — 'I'm afraid to . . .', 'What if . . .?', 'I'm afraid of what might happen if . . .' Let's ask ourselves the questions, 'Why am I afraid to change? What is it that prevents me from doing what I really want?' Identifying the fear is the first step to making that change.

One of the greatest fears for us all is the fear of growing old and moving into the unknown. Every day, we are a day older from the moment we are born. Some of us cope with milestones better than others. Most people find 'turning thirty' pretty devastating, while 'turning forty . . . or fifty . . . or sixty . . .' can create even deeper fears — particularly if you are not adhering to 'society's norms'.

TURNING THE TIDE

Moving into a new decade in our lives undoubtedly brings with it new fears. We do, however, have a choice about how we respond. Basically, we all have to be comfortable with ourselves. For example, society does not expect someone to start a university degree course at the age of sixty. Some people would think it is a waste of time. But for others, it is a new challenge. They get enjoyment from studying and it gives them a new sense of achievement. The whole point of doing anything is to enjoy what you are doing at the moment you are doing it.

A lot of people spend their time talking about what they will do in the future — when they are thirty, forty or fifty. But they never manage to achieve their aims because they are so stressed out by that time that they've lost the energy. Also, in some ways, destiny plays a part. There are certain things over which we have no control. However, if you keep yourself physically and mentally tuned in, you can learn to deal with any eventuality at any age.

CONFRONTATION

Confronting a situation proves a difficult task for most of us. Generally, we try and avoid rather than confront. But sometimes the fear of the confrontation can be worse than the actual head-on meeting itself. We magnify the fear in our minds to such an extent that we can sometimes isolate ourselves totally.

Take the situation of a friend who has wrongly accused you. Should you decide to confront that person, perhaps the following plan might help:

Write down what that person has said to you and how you feel about it. Then perhaps write down how you think you might reply. Then try to anticipate what they might say to you in return. At this stage, if you are on your own and not feeling too confident about your plan, call a friend and explain what it is you want to say. You might even consider doing some role play and rehearsing a little script together to help build your confidence.

Most likely, your friend will diffuse a lot of your fears and you will realise that you have perhaps been oversensitive and built up the fear in your own mind. When you and your friend have sorted out what is the most appropriate and best conversation to have, decide on a time that would suit you and the person involved. Perhaps ask the person over to your house (you'll feel more in control on your own ground) and explain your sentiments about the whole affair in a non-threatening manner. Certainly when it's done, you will feel relieved. You will have diffused your fear and it will give you the confidence to cope in similar situations in the future.

There is no doubt that we have to practise making changes in our lives. They should not be once-off situations but part of a new way of being that suits you better. It is also important to learn to recognise the feeling involved when you are afraid. Ask yourself, is it a feeling of anger or guilt or just self-criticism?

Finally, if you do feel good about your achievement, reward yourself! Build up an empire of little changes. Remember real change takes time and then you must face the fear of how you will cope with the 'new you' even as you are changing.

THE WAY FORWARD

- Start by listing your fears. You don't have to show them to anybody — just write them down and then you can burn them if you want.

- Now try again — I'll guarantee you, the second time around is not so bad. Leave it for a week and read your list again. It won't seem anything as formidable.

- Ask yourself: Are your fears linked to past experiences which represent failures to you? Or are they based on realistic facts of a current situation? Or are they abstract fears of what things might be like in the future?

- Now, take one fear and decide you are going to work on it. Perhaps get a friend to support you in conquering this fear.

CHAPTER 5

ALL ALONE:

Loss and Loneliness

Picture a little girl in a supermarket separated from her parents, surrounded by lots of people yet terrified because she doesn't recognise anyone. You can almost see the fear in her eyes because she is lost, helpless and living in the unknown. She is unsupported and needs reassurance. For many adults, life can be like this. They are unable to articulate what is wrong. They feel afraid that someone may never find them. They feel unsupported. They feel all alone.

This fear of being all alone probably started out for many of us when we were children. Perhaps you did actually get lost one day and this was the first time you felt really alone. Or maybe it was during the afternoon when your parents went out and left you in the house on your own.

Most of us came into the world surrounded by family and friends. It is very important for a child to feel secure and supported. Some feel more supported than others, depending on their circumstances. However, as we grow older many of us carry within us that child-like feeling of being lost.

This may be apparent, for example, the first time you move out of your family home — leaving the nest, as it were. You suddenly feel without family support. Your fear is about taking on responsibility for yourself, responsibility that society expects of you.

Some of us cope much better than others with leaving home and feel ready for this step. Some of us feel so afraid that we delay and find excuses not to do it. Basically, what we are not dealing with is the loss or the changes in the family support network.

LOSS OF BELONGINGS

Loss can be apparent in many other situations. Let's take an example — you are sitting in a hotel and suddenly discover your bag is gone. This is obviously a feeling of loss: you are without the keys of your home, the keys of your car, your personal papers. However, there is also a deeper sense of loss — a feeling of insecurity and confusion. The situation is out of your control. You feel frightened and afraid of what might happen next.

There is also a strong feeling of loss if somebody burglars your home — the loss of personal belongings, the loss of things that you had treasured. You then live in the house afraid that somebody might break in again and you feel you have lost your own private space.

LOSS OF JOB

When you are young and just finished school, you are delighted that your examinations are over and that you have the freedom to be independent, to look for a job. Most people look forward to having their own job and money. However, few of us are prepared for losses that might happen at an early stage, for example, the loss of a job. Once we get a job, we think we are on the road to success, the road to monetary gain and even fame for some people.

If you got your job quite easily, you may be confident that you will never have any difficulties. But today we live in a climate where no one can be totally secure in their jobs and protected from the feelings that loss of a job can bring to a person at any age. For many, it is not just losing the job that matters: it is also the loss of status and economic independence. It can lead ultimately to the loss of material goods such as your car and even your home.

Losing your job affects people differently and can alter our philosophy about life and status. For example, if a man loses his job and has always been the breadwinner of the family, he may now have to alter his role, change his lifestyle and stay at home.

The biggest fear in all of this is that perhaps you will never work again. You feel like you've been rejected not only by your organisation but by society. You feel that you have nothing to offer or that your contribution is not worthwhile. The unbearable grief and loss can lead to other problems like stress and an inability to face up to interviews. This can have tragic effects in that some people can feel suicidal when they lose their job. When this happens, there is a double problem and the person really needs help.

It is very important that no matter what loss we have experienced, we don't turn it into a double blow and lose other things as a result.

For example, you may have been working very diligently in a company, but due to the economic climate the company has had to cut back. Okay, so you know that you have lost your job, but you also know that you have ability and that with patience, time and effort you will get another one.

However, some people become so devastated that the loss

becomes a double loss and they lose their ability and confidence to apply themselves. They opt out of any leisure activities because they feel they are only valued for their work and not for anything else. They could lose a relationship because they become so depressed that their partner finds them too difficult to cope with.

Nobody likes having to deal with loss of any kind, but you have to get things in perspective. It is important to look at the positive rather than the negative side of the situation and prioritise. This is why it is important that if you suffer a loss, you talk to someone and get support to deal with it effectively. Coping with the loss, rather than multiplying and developing other losses, is the only way of dealing with the original problem.

DEATH

The biggest loss of all is the loss of a friend or relative due to death. For some, this loss is so traumatic that the healing takes years. It is difficult even to articulate the words for how you feel. People around you don't know what to say or do.

Your fear is that you will not be able to cope without this person in your life again. You are afraid that you will be left alone like this, that you will never be cared for again or that you will never love someone else again.

Feelings of loss have nothing to do with age. Just like the lost child, a widower in old age can feel that same sense of loss and fear. Loss and loneliness are very closely linked. A person who constantly feels very lonely does in a way also feel very lost.

There is a big difference between being alone and feeling loneliness. Some of us enjoy being alone. We enjoy the sense of peace, the sense of independence, the time to ourselves, the space to relax in. Others are unable to enjoy these situations and find being alone unbearable.

Being alone can, in fact, be unbearable, especially if you've experienced the loss of a close companion or a partner. You can experience a strong sense of loss — the loss of the person you were close to, the loneliness of being on your own and then the fear that nothing will ever change.

RELATIONSHIPS

While death or loss of health are the most devastating blows, the breaking up of a relationship can have an enormous impact on us. We can feel the loss to such an extent that we lose all sense of value and self-esteem, our health is affected, we become stressed and lose sight of who we are. We feel almost as if part of ourselves has been cut off because we feel so alone.

If this happens, you lose total confidence in yourself because you feel no one else will want you. Not only do you feel rejected by your ex-partner, but you start to reject yourself for having been rejected — which is, of course, a double blow. Your home becomes a mess and you start to isolate yourself. Your friends lose interest in you because you even lose your sense of humour. Losses such as these pile up and what eventually happens is the original problem is no longer clear. You have lost the core of the problem and have no energy left to cope and no support left to call upon.

LONELINESS

Loneliness can exist for people when they are in a crowd or even when they are in a relationship. This type of loneliness can be deeper because as far as everyone else is concerned, the person is surrounded by people and no one can recognise what they are feeling.

To feel lonely in a crowd can be very sad. It can be very isolating. It is a very frightening experience and yet in many ways, the greatest sadness is that no one around you realises your dilemma.

Going through such pain, loss and fear on your own can be traumatic. People sometimes feel desperate in these situations and the worst feeling of all is that things will never move on, that they will never change.

INDEPENDENCE

Some people have a marvellous ability to portray a sense of being able to cope on their own and of being independent. But their problem could be the fear of losing that independence, together with the fear of making a commitment. This is more relevant when you are in a relationship: problems can occur when you or your partner decide to get involved only to a certain extent and pull out at the last minute because of this fear of losing personal independence and freedom.

CHILDREN

However, for those who do make the commitment other losses may occur in their lives. For many having made the big step and committed themselves to each other, the next step is having children. This cannot be taken for granted since some couples discover that they are unable to have children. The loss of the child they never had can be as significant as the loss of a child due to cot death or a tragic accident.

For such couples, grieving can be more difficult because they have never had the pleasure of announcing the arrival of their child, or even living with the child for a short time in the case of a cot death. They may also find it very difficult to talk about their sadness to friends or relatives, and can be subjected to remarks such as 'No sign of the patter of little feet yet, is there?' They often feel tongue-tied when they try to explain that they cannot have children.

The loss of a child is an horrific experience. It is traumatic for both parents and also for brothers and sisters. There are other types of loss: there's the loss for the couple unable to have a child of their own, and there's the loss for a single person who has never met 'that special person' with whom they could have children.

Regardless of what the situation is, the loss for each person and the grief they endure is unique to them. In all situations, people must be allowed the time and the space to heal and to grieve at their own pace. There is no right or wrong way to approach grieving and everyone finds a way that suits them best. Some people may never get over certain losses and actually live to the end of their days with a grief that they learn to cope with.

It is important we recognise loss for what it is. Unless we deal with the signals, the pain of the loss, the anxiety and the stress, we can multiply all the losses to such an extent that we feel as if we could almost end up losing everything.

THE WAY FORWARD

- Acknowledge your loss.

- Recognise that you can get help and support, and share your loss with someone else.

- Deal with the initial loss rather than multiplying your problems.

- Realise that it will take some time to get over your loss. Give yourself time and be patient and kind with yourself.

CHAPTER 6

KICK THE HABIT:
Do you want to change?

Why is it that when we start out enjoying something — like a bar of chocolate, a cigarette, shopping for clothes or a nice cool alcoholic drink — it can end up as a 'bad habit' and we feel we need to give it up.

For some people, bad habits become more than just bad habits. They become addictions. People who smoke never intend to get hooked on cigarettes. They usually start off by just having one or two with friends and never buying a packet. Then gradually, they start buying packs of ten and sooner than they'd like to admit, they are smoking more and more every day. Before they know it, their habit has become a dependency which later becomes an addiction. No matter how hard they try, they cannot give it up.

ADDICTION

Once a habit becomes an addiction, it is very difficult to deal with. Not only does it affect you but it can, particularly in the case of alcoholism, affect those around you. Drinking a bottle of gin a day or several pints of beer not only kills thousands of your brain cells and weakens your liver, but it also affects your psychological well-being, making you less capable of doing your job and being able to manage your life. It has knock-on effects on your family and friends, and on your employers too in that they have to cope with your destructive behaviour.

Addiction creates chaos and turmoil in your life and 'kicking the habit' can become a full-time occupation in itself. You may end up on a merry-go-round of trying to break the habit only to realise that it is a greater problem than you thought. Some individuals, on drugs or alcohol, have to reach rock bottom before they go for help.

It is only when you look closely at what you are doing that you can learn you are fulfilling a deep-seated need for comfort. The addiction in many cases is only the symptom of the problem and that can only be dealt with if the source of the problem is confronted.

SIGNALS

Sometimes there are signals that prompt you to do something about your habit. However, more often than not, you fail to heed them. No one is born with a need to smoke or drink or take pep pills, but some circumstances can lead you to get hooked. Let's look at what could be happening and how your crutch can become a living nightmare.

Allowing yourself to become overtired at work, to the extent that you become exhausted, can lead you to a physical and mental low. You feel like you need a crutch to carry on. What you really need is sleep, but you convince yourself that you are indispensable in work and you solve your problem by having a drink or an 'upper' pill.

You may feel like you have solved your initial problem, but you can end up going down the road of dependency and complete exhaustion. This could perhaps be followed by 'rationalising' — in other words, making excuses for not doing what you have to do and doing what you know you shouldn't be doing.

MERRY-GO-ROUND

This type of merry-go-round can lead you into living a life of lies, deceits and dishonesty. Your 'crutch' — be it food, alcohol or drugs — has become more important to you than living. A part of you wants to hide the reality of what you are doing from everyone else.

You become argumentative. You feel everybody is unreasonable with you and you feel frustrated because they don't agree with you or follow your way. You start to expect too much from others and you are constantly asking why can't people do things your way. You are impatient with your family and friends.

You feel things are not happening fast enough for you. However, you do believe you are coping. Are you? Perhaps you are only doing so through a mask of defences. If you let down your guard, all will be revealed. Perhaps, deep down, you lack confidence, you feel insecure and that life is not going the way you want it to.

While your little habit started out by giving you a kick in the right direction, what you now need to do is to kick your habit which has grown into an addiction. When the dependency becomes more than the crutch, other areas of your life fall apart and you lose sight of who you really are. What was once important to you — your family, friends, work and finance — now means nothing.

Your 'fix' is now the most important thing in your life. The sad thing is that you know you are still on that merry-go-round, but now you feel you can't get off. Perhaps you have gone down the road so far that your isolation and loneliness leaves you even further away from the answers and ties you up more with your habit.

Friends may want to reach out and help you. But the more they do, the more you push them away. This is the most painful aspect of an addiction — when you are surrounded by people who want to help and you are running away in the opposite direction.

For some, it is not until they reach rock bottom that they are ready to confront their problem. With professional help, some people can change their lifestyle and even give up their habit. This is only possible if they tune in to themselves and are willing to make changes that will ultimately make their life happier.

Others, unfortunately, find it more difficult to reach the road of recovery. They have to fall many times before they are ready to pick up the pieces.

CRUTCH

Addictive behaviour can come in many guises. No one sets out to be labelled 'an addict' of any sort, but it is very important to recognise the signs that send you heading for your 'crutch'. If you can become aware of these signs in the early stages, you could prevent yourself from going down the thorny road of addiction.

Addictive behaviour can creep up on you subtly and at any age. Very often, extreme loneliness, exhaustion and deep-seated insecurities can be the real reasons why you reach out for your crutch. None of us can afford the luxury of saying 'It could never happen to me'. Above all, you must become aware of what it is you could turn to when things are not going well. Is it cigarettes? drugs? alcohol? overspending? food? constantly wanting to telephone someone to talk?

If, in some way, your crutch is interfering with your life and has become a bad habit, it is time you started to 'kick the habit' before it 'kicks you'.

THE WAY FORWARD

- Admit to yourself that your habit is more that just a bad habit and that it is upsetting your life and those around you.

- Spend time with people who do not encourage you to continue your bad habit and who give you support to do other things.

- Be patient and kind to yourself while trying to kick your habit.

- Avoid isolating yourself and becoming overtired and stressed out.

CHAPTER 7

TUNNEL VISION:
Widening your horizons

We all want things in life that we have no way of getting —
things we've always dreamt of but see no way of acquiring.
Instead of feeling like some day we will achieve our goals, we
feel like our lives are leading us down a dark tunnel which
seems to have no light.

People say to you things like 'You should widen your horizons' or 'If only you could see beyond your personal circumstances'. But the problem is you don't even know where
your horizons are. At times, you wish there was a hole which
would swallow you up and help you to forget your entire
existence.

LOW SELF-WORTH

Have you ever experienced the sensation of being hemmed in, like being in a tunnel with no light or movement. For example, the day you felt totally rejected by someone who had been close to you or the day you lost your job or the day it was confirmed that you had a serious illness.

The image of the tunnel can be quite frightening. It leaves you with a sense of isolation, fear and powerlessness. Sometimes you can get so low that you wonder if life is worth living at all. Different circumstances can cause you to react in these ways and at the time you feel so powerless that life seems to be just passing you by. Somehow, the dread of getting out of this tunnel can be as bad as the pain of staying in because, in some ways, you have lost all sense of hope and your self-esteem has dropped to an all-time low.

People who suffer from extremely low self-esteem and low self-worth can identify with the image of the tunnel even though those around them seem to be beacons of light, encouraging them on. In such cases, the light only dazzles them, making them want to shield themselves and move further into the darkness.

For those looking on, it can also be difficult because they feel powerless trying to coax their friend or partner out of the darkness. They don't have the words or the language to put things in perspective, but they sense that it is not good to grope around in the darkness for too long.

When someone is feeling this low, people reminding them of better times can have the opposite effect and make them feel even more negative. It seems nothing will stir them.

Sometimes the individual may need to stand still and just experience the pain until they feel exhausted by their own inertia. Like a crumble of earth in a tunnel, any little thing can suddenly shift them from their useless feelings, such as an unexpected gift, phone call or letter. It is only then that they start to want to move forwards.

Initially you take small steps, half wanting to go back into the darkness and sink lower. But with time and support from those

around you, you can move on at your own pace, leaving behind
your sense of deep sadness and isolation.

OUT OF THE DARKNESS

When you start to move out of such darkness, it is like learning
to walk again. You take one step and you fall down. You may
even hurt again and wonder if it is worth the effort. At times,
you think you felt safer in the dark tunnel. While being uncomfortable, it was more familiar than this new light ahead. Coming
from dark to light can be daunting. The fear of not being able to
go back is always there.

As you take further steps forwards and stand up, you realise
that, like a child, you are doing it on your own. Each day brings
new progress. The end point will be reached sooner or later,
depending on the severity of your sadness or pain.

For some people, recovering from severe sadness can take
time. The main thing is that when you start to move, you
recognise that any sign of movement is a sign of progress and
healing. In other words, you are getting better. It is only when
you reach the end of your tunnel that you can begin to widen
your horizons.

If you have survived the challenge of the tunnel, you will now
be prepared to grapple with new experiences, take new risks and
start to enjoy the rest of your life. There will be days when you
wonder how you could ever have been in the tunnel at all. Other
times, you may pick up a diary or an old photograph which
reminds you of these days, although you barely recognise yourself. In fact, you can become so well that you can eventually
forget the pain.

Fortunately, many people remain in the light, maintaining
their sense of well-being through good open communication
about their feelings. Others turn to counselling and therapy for
help during the dark, stressful times.

Other people experience the light, but unfortunately don't
have sufficient knowledge or support to stay there. Not knowing

how to cope with new situations may send them shrinking back into the darkness. But often, having experienced new horizons, albeit briefly, they may feel subconsciously that the second trip 'up the tunnel' is not worth it. Their expectations and deeper needs may no longer be met there. They may not need to go in as deeply as before and can come out more quickly the second time around.

Some people's tunnel isn't as long or as deep, and they can reach the light more quickly once it is shone on them. In fact, all they needed was a helping hand and perhaps somebody to show them the way forwards. For them, the tunnel represents a fear of venturing into new areas that they believe they won't be able to cope with or feel free to grow in.

Many of us create small tunnels that we can escape into when things get on top of us. Our tunnels give us security and warmth where we don't have to expose our true selves.

TIME OUT

Sometimes what we need is simply 'time out'. Our engines are not burnt out, but they need refuelling. Certain situations in our lives can create so-called 'tunnel vision'. For example, in times of stress we can find ourselves reacting negatively to things that we would normally thrive on. Let's take an example.

John is an executive in a large organisation. He enjoys his job and generally thrives on the buzz of his department. However, at certain times of the year, it can all get too much for him. He feels compelled to keep up with his colleagues and the strong sense of competitiveness with other firms makes him nervous. While he still piles in the extra hours, he feels he can't cope. He begins to feel stressed out. He can't think straight. He doesn't sleep at night and all he really wants to do is to curl up in a dark place and hibernate.

Perhaps this is what he has to do to survive the high-flying executive lifestyle he finds himself leading. The reason this may have happened is that John didn't know how to pace himself.

He didn't prioritise things that were important. He never listened to what his body was really telling him.

Instead of getting the normal eight hours of sleep and three meals a day, he was living on four hours of sleep and grabbing junk food here and there. Perhaps he even found certain things like alcohol kept him going. But all this was doing was bringing him further down.

Many of us are fooled into thinking that we can keep going on very little sleep, no exercise and an inadequate diet. We may think we have superhuman bodies, but nature inevitably takes over and we collapse under the strain. No one is superhuman.

THE WAY FORWARD

- Recognise what for you is a stressful situation.

- Look at your reactions — mentally, physically and emotionally — to these situations and to the circumstances that threaten you.

- Realise that even if you feel low, it can't last forever.

- Learn how to deal with your moods and swings by acknowledging them and giving yourself some 'time out' if necessary.

CHAPTER 8

STUCK IN A RUT:

Mobilize yourself

Picture yourself and your daily routine. You get up, take a shower and have your breakfast. You go into work following the same traffic route, park your car in the same place or get off your bus at the same stop, seeing the same people start their day in the same way as yourself.

You go to your workplace and begin your day at the same time every day, noting the hours and minutes until your coffee break. You talk to the same people at coffee and lunch breaks, all of you discussing more or less the same things. Later, you go home, reasonably content but minorly bored by your daily routine.

You find yourself saying things like — 'If only I didn't live in Ireland . . . If I lived in Australia, things would be much better' or 'If I wasn't married to John or Mary, my life would be more exciting . . .'

ROUTINE

Routine is unavoidable in our everyday lives. But when you begin to feel that you are just filling in the time, whether at work or in your home life, perhaps it is time to take a look at what is going on. Are you perhaps stuck in a rut?

Stuck in a rut can mean many things: you may be stuck in a flat you don't want to be in, you may be stuck in a neighbour-hood that you can't stand, you may be stuck in a job that is leading nowhere, you may be stuck in a relationship that is suffocating you. The reality is that you want to break free from a situation that you feel trapped in.

For some, it is a simple case of being bored, needing a new challenge, stimulation or excitement. If this is the case, you can realise that your 'stuck in a rut' syndrome is mere boredom and that you are choosing to be bored. You can just as easily choose to get out of this situation by doing something different.

WHAT DO YOU REALLY WANT?

The starting point is to recognise what it is that makes you feel like this. Then acknowledge it, feel it and admit to yourself that you want to get out. For those of us who can, we then have to look at options and ask ourselves 'What do I really want?'

If you think it is your job that makes you feel 'stuck in a rut' and somebody comes along and offers you an alternative which you turn down, then perhaps the job is not the problem at all; it is *you* who is stuck with yourself. Maybe it is your inner self you need to change, your attitude to something or your leisure life which is void.

Similarly, if you are in a relationship which is going nowhere, you need the courage to confront the situation, break free and perhaps go through a period of living alone before you are ready to meet someone else.

For many of us, staying stuck in a rut is an option. While you might bore everyone else by saying it, the reality is that in some way staying stuck is preferable to breaking free and feeling abandoned. If this is the case and you feel totally unable to break loose, you can always make changes within your own circumstances.

Some people find it frightening to acknowledge that they have a choice about something because it means that they have to choose to give up something else. It is this giving up something else that can actually prove most difficult. You wonder if you will cope with your new situation.

The biggest problem people have is that they get stuck in the whole routine of their lives and then, unless they reach a crisis point, they won't change.

SMALL CHANGES

Getting into the habit of making small changes in your life can make it easier to think about making a bigger one. You are also getting to know what you do like by changing some things.

For example, if it is your flat or house that is the problem and you genuinely can't afford to move, you can always repaint the place, change around the furniture or redesign a room. Make changes that get you out of that 'stuck in a rut' feeling.

While you may feel stuck geographically, you can, for example, decide to have 'treat days' for yourself and get away from the situation. In the end, it is about learning to make changes and creating new situations that give you the freedom to try new experiences which will widen your horizons.

Being stuck can occur at any time in your life. Some people get stuck at a very early age and it becomes the driving force for them to climb the ladder of success. Others label it 'the mid-life crisis', when they feel they really have to take stock. They may have spent 20 years living life in a certain way and now feel 'I'm not able to change although I no longer feel happy like this'. There is no right or wrong age for people to feel stuck and to have the ability to unstick themselves.

If you find yourself thinking or saying 'I'm stuck in a rut', this is the signal to change. But you will only change when you really want to. If you find yourself using these words and not doing anything, perhaps you may have to accept that there is a part of you that enjoys the feeling.

Some of us feel that we only 'exist' in this life. We don't feel alive or that we are really enjoying ourselves. We are constantly making excuses for the situations we are in with comments like 'If only things were different, I wouldn't be here'. We survive by day-dreaming and envying other people's lives.

To change from your situation, you may have to risk changing your attitude and a way of living that has become a life-long habit. You have to risk in order to change. Ask yourself, 'Am I prepared for this?'

Some people are stuck in a way that they have wrapped themselves up in protective cotton wool. But in fact they are really wrapped up in self-hatred and negative thoughts that stick to them like glue. Sometimes they are even loyal to these negative thoughts.

HABITS

Like any habit, being stuck in a rut is not easy to give up. Some people would feel they couldn't handle life if they gave up their crutch which is usually the incentive or pay-off for staying stuck. The big question is — 'Do you want to change?'

If you do, you have to become unstuck at every level in your life. Initially, you have to start changing your thinking. Then you must alter aspects of your belief system which have kept you stuck in such a way that you dislike yourself. And you have to start listening to what's going on inside you.

THE WAY FORWARD

- Admit that you are stuck in a rut.

- Define what your rut is — your home? your job? your relationship? your family? yourself?

- Decide what it is you want to change and make a decision to change one small part — for example, while thinking of moving flat or house, start by making small changes in your own home.

- Keep two lists: one with the changes you make and another with the rewards you will give yourself — your own treatment programme. Always be conscious when you achieve something that (a) you feel good about it and (b) you reward yourself in some way. This will stimulate you to continue.

CHAPTER 9

DON'T PUT YOUR FOOT IN IT:
Appropriate and inappropriate beliefs

Have you ever heard the phrase 'Don't put your foot in it' ringing in your ears and yet in a funny way, you continue to say things that most definitely prove you are capable of doing just that.

What exactly do we mean by 'putting your foot in it'? Let's take an example: Mary works in the local shop and has recently got engaged to a man from India. A customer comes in and, noticing her beautiful engagement ring, congratulates her and asks her how did she meet her fiancée.

Mary explains that her fiancée was living in a house close by, belonging to a friend of hers. The customer comments, 'Oh isn't that wonderful, marrying 'the boy next door' instead of a for-eigner like a lot of young women do these days'. Fortunately, Mary has a sense of humour and sees the funny side of how the customer has 'put his foot in it'. However, the customer is oblivious of this and goes on his thoughtless way. If Mary hadn't had such a good attitude towards the event, she might have felt very hurt and humiliated by his comment.

SOCIAL NORMS

Let's look at what really went on here: the customer was inter-preting what Mary said in his own mind. He was using his own value system to decide what was good or bad for Mary. In other words, the customer felt that it was healthy, acceptable and appropriate that Mary should marry somebody local, one of her own kind, 'the boy next door'. Mary, on the other hand, has her own value system and considers the quality of the relationship more important than adhering to the social norms.

Some people are very concerned about what other people say or do, and think that if they are acting according to what they think are acceptable social norms, they are then valued in the eyes of onlookers. For example, people who place a lot of impor-tance on etiquette may always have the 'correct' behaviour, but they may not value friendship and instead consider somebody wearing the correct attire more important than somebody who has put themselves out for a friend. They operate on one level only — they value appearances, but never look beyond.

On the other hand, there are people who go overboard and rebel against social norms; they may feel that to adhere to society's norms is giving in to authority. They almost go out of their way not to do what society expects of them. This sort of behaviour can upset other people.

MATURITY

What we really should be aiming for is a sense of balance in being able to accept cultural and religious norms, yet to have the maturity to have our own sense of values. Maturity is about being able to decide or recognise what value system you want to apply to yourself that will not damage others.

For some people, religious beliefs can help them to decide on their value system, for example by following a defined set of rules. But other people find it difficult to adhere to a particular belief system. They may find through the struggle of living that they construct their own set of rules to help them live a better life.

It is much easier to go through life not having to work all this out because when something goes wrong, you can always blame someone else. In other words, you will always hear the voice of someone else ringing in your ears when you don't like what is going on for you. For example, you can blame your mother or father, the system, your schooling or even the culture you live in.

Some people go through a stage of rebelling against the system — usually during their teenage years — and come away from this as stronger people for having worked out their own ideas. Other people may work things out for themselves at a later stage — perhaps in their thirties — and others live life according to a set of rules laid down by their families, teachers or employers without ever working out whether they suit them or not.

VALUE SYSTEMS

Many people survive 'systems' by learning to manipulate them. When we learn to manipulate something, we learn to go all around the issue. In so doing, we waste a lot of energy instead of going to the core of something and confronting it head-on which would clarify things and allow us to perform much better. However, there is a risk of losing everything in the process.

Sadly, many people don't learn about value systems until they are thrust upon them in work or in a relationship. Before that, they drift along, surviving in this way without really confronting anything. It takes a lot of courage to question your value system, your belief system and your social norms.

To take a stand on something can be difficult. Say you disagree with something because you think it is morally wrong, dishonest or going to hurt someone else. You may be alienated by others who would rather go with the flow and you might find it painful that nobody supports your values on a certain issue. However, remember we all have to live with ourselves and if you can have the courage of your convictions, you will be the stronger person for it, provided your convictions are appropriate and have good foundations.

However, we must not confuse having your own values with taking a stand on issues for the sake of standing out or drawing attention to yourself. For example, if you discover from the first time you stand out on issues that you get attention, you may begin to seek this attention more than you seek the resolution of the issues. You could learn a new way of behaving from this, but you must decide whether it is worthwhile or not.

The key to accepting your own set of values is to sound them out and see how they work for you without upsetting somebody else. When we say something that is unacceptable to someone else and in some way realise that we have hurt them, it may be a case of 'putting your foot in it'. But if it is the first occurrence, it may be just a way of testing the waters because we know the next time to be more circumspect.

People who are constantly 'putting their foot in it' are never learning from their mistakes. In a way, they have become restricted by their own value system because they never learn to modify it. Manipulative or cunning people may use the expression 'Oh, I've put my foot in it again' as a way of excusing their own inability to accept behaviour outside their norms.

MISTAKES

Most people learn by their mistakes. In other words, when they put their foot in it, they realise that they have done so and are

mature enough to recognise that they were the cause of creating
the ripple; they learn from their mistake and don't do it again.

Some people find it very difficult to change their own value
system. People who have very strong traditional beliefs — cultural, religious or family — may sometimes feel uncomfortable
about certain issues, but they are afraid to embrace new situations for fear of severe consequences. They feel in some way
that they will be punished and this can create a lot of stress in
their lives.

Such people feel that if they embrace another value system,
they have 'let the side down' and that their whole world will
collapse about them. They feel that in such a situation, they will
have no support to rebuild it.

Sometimes, people's struggle to adhere to certain belief systems has led to violence. And other people, while they appear
to behave in a certain way or to be adhering to a set of rules,
actually have their own inner aggression tearing them apart.
While they appear very passive, inside there is a louder message
of aggression and people in their company feel victimised, even
though the person is coming across as non-aggressive.

FITTING IN

Some people's belief systems are so strong that they think within
a one-way system. While they have very strong moral beliefs,
they also have a strong need to conform and follow the social
norms that they believe in. They want other people to accept
their value system, yet in many ways they are holding on to it
like a lifebelt. Let go of it and they would feel worthless.

What is in fact happening is that they see their value system
as a means of controlling others. They only welcome people who
are going to fit into their system. They only need one person to
be different for them to feel totally threatened. Their longing to
belong is confused with what real value systems are about. Their
scales would become totally unbalanced if somebody pressed
the wrong button. Sometimes, these people are actually very

vulnerable and their ability to control others gives them power, a false sense of security and a means of never confronting what is really going on in their own lives.

Mature people learn to balance appropriate norms related to cultural, religious and family values with their own personal needs. It is a never-ending journey. No one ever reaches a point of completion, but that is, of course, the challenge of life.

THE WAY FORWARD

- Get to know your own value system.

- Learn to be flexible in your thinking.

- Value your own beliefs as well as others.

- Remember, life continues to present you with new challenges.

CHAPTER 10

INSTITUTION or INTUITION:

Resources and coping techniques

Most people are born into a family unit which is their first sense
of being a member of an institution. The sense of belonging to
this institution of the family is usually a good experience. It
allows you to learn about discipline and structure. It guides you
in such a way that you can learn to develop as a worthwhile
human being, with the freedom to be intuitive, talented and
move in the direction that you choose.

PEER PRESSURE

From the family unit, we generally move into our next institution, namely the primary school. Here our experience can be very different. We become slightly more institutionalised and we have to adhere more to norms and social structures. Peer pressure makes us question ourselves and teachers can either stifle our talent or encourage us to use our skills to the full. However, it is our secondary school experience (depending on the particular type of school or teachers) which allows us to develop and explore ourselves.

FREEDOM

Freedom for the individual means being allowed to be intuitive, original and able to listen to our gut feelings. It is also about being able to solve problems, find solutions and take responsibility for our own lives. Some of us come through the teenage years ready to do this, others emerge confused. These years can be filled with ups and downs, highs and lows, and the ability to make decisions can come slowly.

At the end of our teenage years, we brace ourselves for adulthood. At this stage, we usually enter new organisations (companies, universities, etc) which become new institutions. These organisations either empower or disempower us. An organisation which empowers us allows us to display our talents and initiative, while also using our sense of intuition. This means that we can perform to the best of our ability, allowing others to learn from us and vica versa.

INSTITUTIONALISED

An organisation that disempowers the individual makes us feel trapped. Many of us get sucked into the system where we spend our time moaning, blaming others and demeaning ourselves.

We lose our own sense of selves in the institution. We become sucked into the negative aspects of the institution. We lose our sense of freedom and our sense of fun.

In such environments, issues like powerplay, bullying and manipulation become the order of the day and people become so fearful to break loose from this (by, for example, saying you disagree with something) that it is often easier to become institutionalised than it is to break free.

Unfortunately, many of us don't realise this is happening. We are so glad to have a job that we are afraid to question anything. Our self-worth plummets. Other aspects of our lives, such as our relationships with family and friends, may suffer at the same time. But we cannot see what the real problem is — we have become institutionalised.

Usually, it is such a long process that you don't notice it happening. While the coffee break may seem like relief from your job, it may, in fact, be the very symbol of being institutionalised. You sit with the same people, you become one of them again, you all complain about your jobs, without ever being aware of how you are behaving.

Many of us start out wanting to be part of an institution. We think it will give us money, security, a pension. Sadly, some of us may never live to see our pension (due to such uncontrollable factors as redundancies, take-overs, death), while others will successfully manage to recognise what the institution is and put it in perspective.

Not only can you become institutionalised in your work, but also in your relationships. What happens is you no longer bring a sense of freedom or fun to what you do. You become stale. There are days when you get glimpses that you want to break free. Your role in the family can even become institutionalised. What you do may be taken for granted. When your role becomes greater than yourself, you have lost your sense of self. What you have to do is to stop, look and listen to what others are saying and learn what it is that you should really be contributing.

Nobody ever goes around saying such things as 'I feel institutionalised'. You say things like 'I'm bored', 'I'm fed up', 'I feel trapped', 'I feel suffocated', 'I want to get out but I don't know how', 'I'm afraid if I step out of line. . . .', 'I'm afraid if I say what I really feel. . . .' At times, you feel almost numb because you are not being valued, without realising that you are possibly not contributing anything either.

In some ways, you want to return to the way you were when you started out in the institution. You were versatile, original, you felt needed, you were wanted, you were valued. You were flavour of the month. Now, you realise you are none of these things and you wonder what has gone wrong.

YOU HAVE A CHOICE

To survive, you have choices. You can break free of your job and move on to something else. To do this, you have to start thinking differently about yourself. You may also have to change your way of life.

There are always alternative routes. There are always options. Don't get yourself buried under the rubble of the institution. Life is too short for this. Break free. It may be painful initially, but you can always do it step by step.

In order to avoid being institutionalised, you must remind yourself of the person you are. Perhaps you could even note down all the positive things you have contributed to the institution and if this job or relationship doesn't suit you any longer, remember you always have the choice to leave or change your behaviour within it.

Your intuition is greater than the institution. It gives you the ability to listen to your gut feelings, to be able to reason and to be able to find solutions. If you suppress your intuition, you will lose part of yourself. But if you leave an institution, you can move on to new experiences, a more mature person who is sensitive to his or her own needs for happiness and fulfilment.

RELIEF SYSTEM

In order to give yourself relief from a system that weighs you down, perhaps you should try to develop another side to your life through new associations or activities.

One aspect of your life can sometimes dominate all others — for example, your job — and the development of something which releases creativity or stretches your potential could be the first step in giving you new freedom. Why not consider doing something completely different? If you are a 'sporty' type, why not try an artistic hobby — take up painting or pottery or photography, for example. If, on the other hand, you are an 'indoor' type, given to reading or other types of 'lone' pursuits, why not try being more social — join a club or association where you can meet people with similar hobbies and exchange views.

VALUE YOURSELF

To avoid becoming institutionalised in your work or in your relationships, you must constantly keep abreast of what is really going on. If there is something you don't like, you have to be able to step back and say, 'I am part of this, but I don't like it and I value myself more than the institution'.

You may have to learn to detach yourself from your work and place more value on your relationships. You may have to leave the institution to get back your freedom. You may even have to move from where you live to revalue yourself.

Whatever you do, remember you as a person are greater than any organisation and particularly in relationships, learn to respect and value your own contribution.

THE WAY FORWARD

- Be intuitive — get to know your gut feelings.

- Be prepared to make changes if necessary.

- Try to be creative about what you do.

- Have fun and enjoy yourself — break free from your institutionalised behaviour without losing what you value.

CHAPTER 11

ANXIETY-FREE:

Decision-making and living with the consequences

Do you ever find yourself in situations where you can't make a decision. You want to go one way, but some part of you is afraid and you end up going in a direction you don't really want to go. Perhaps halfway down the road, you realise your mistake, go back and end up in 'no-man's land'.

INDECISION

Indecision can be a very uncomfortable experience. Often it is rooted in fear and anxiety. Anxiety can affect a person's behaviour in several ways. Most of us feel anxious at key moments in our lives — for example at a job interview, before going on stage or making a speech in public, before an examination or going on a date or getting married.

Small levels of anxiety can often stimulate or motivate us to move in a more positive direction. This type of anxiety is, in effect, quite healthy and appropriate. But anxiety which brings on huge doses of indecision can be rooted in deep-seated fear.

Some people feel anxious all the time and they cannot find a logical reason why this is happening. The anxiety affects them in such a way that they live their lives going round in circles without ever finding a gap to lead them towards more worry-free times.

A lot of energy can be wasted trying to overcome this anxiety and the result is usually a lack of activity. Everything seems to pile up. You don't know where to start. Jobs seem too difficult to perform. Arranging a social event ends up with you alienating yourself because you can't decide who you want to be with. For many people, this type of behaviour can even become a bad habit. Anxiety and indecision can also lead to poor concentration and errors in your thinking. Constantly looking at the black side of things and blaming yourself for being this way can only add to the problem. People who worry a lot never allow themselves to enjoy the present and are always predicting worse things to come.

WORRY

Some people even use such language as 'I'm so worried that I can never do anything' (and they usually never do) or 'I'm so worried about such and such, and this is bad for my blood pressure'. Sometimes what you are worried about never happens. The pay-off, however, is that you avoid risks and you give yourself an excuse to do nothing.

You can seek attention in this way, by becoming ill ('I'm worried sick about...'). You may even be perceived as 'a carer'. You may spend your time being anxious about somebody else and never make decisions about your own life. Many of us spend our time reacting to the needs and demands of others. Remember that you are responsible for your own feelings and that friends and partners are not to blame for how you feel.

Basically, worrying about things and not making decisions is linked to inflexible ways of thinking. Some people overgeneralise and predict disaster on every possible occasion. Others see things in a very pessimistic way; for example, if a friend has promised to call to your house at a certain time and hasn't arrived, then you think something terrible must have happened.

There are also the 'born worriers' — those who dwell on something for so long that they can no longer see the real issue. They magnify little incidents into huge catastrophes and jump to conclusions at every chance they get. You have to ask yourself if what you are worrying about is likely to happen or not. Is your thinking rational or irrational? What evidence do you have to support such fears? How would someone else view what you are worrying about? And, finally, does your way of thinking prevent you from getting what you want?

Worrying or feeling anxious about things blurs your vision. Not only does it make you become indecisive and anxious, but it also makes you hypercritical of yourself and others. By not making decisions yourself, you can become bitter towards those who seem to be getting on with their lives.

CRITICISM

People who become very critical of others may escape unhappiness themselves through not making a wrong move. However, they become stuck into a pattern of behaviour which repeats itself without benefit to anyone. Being critical of others may even make you feel important at the expense of others.

Criticism is something none of us enjoy and most of us find difficult to cope with. Unexpected criticism usually makes us cringe inside. If we anticipate criticism, we feel anxious and put up defences against it. If we are feeling a bit low and lacking in self-confidence, even the slightest criticism can have an harsh effect on us. On the other hand, a criticism may be entirely unjustified because the person doing the criticising has their own problems or perhaps they have an hidden agenda in relation to you. All in all, you have to be able to distinguish between the different types of criticism.

Bad memories of being criticized by your parents can make the experience more difficult. For example, if your parents often said things like 'You're stupid' or 'You're untidy', instead of 'That's a stupid thing to do' or 'That was a clumsy way to do that', you may end up feeling more sensitive towards criticism later in life — even when it is valid criticism. Reacting negatively to criticism is linked to the need for approval or the avoidance of disapproval.

Let's look at how to cope with criticism. First, decide whether the criticism you encounter is valid or not (this may take some practice and a lot of honesty). Then if the criticism is valid, accept it and admit it by saying something like 'Yes, you're right, I am untidy', rather than melting into a puddle of despair or screaming 'How dare you'. Remember nobody is perfect and it is only human to have faults. However, it is self-destructive not to be able to admit or accept them.

If the criticism is not valid, you don't have to accept it. Depending on the situation, you can joke or just quietly assert that the criticism is not true. For example, you could say something like 'I'm sorry but that is not true' or 'I don't accept that'.

Following these three simple steps can help you understand better how to deal with criticism. Rejecting invalid criticism can make you feel more powerful, while accepting valid criticism is part of being honest with yourself, which ultimately leads to a healthier way of life.

THE WAY FORWARD

- Make a special effort to be more decisive.
- Keep life simple — don't give others free accommodation in your head.
- Decide now to stop worrying unnecessarily.
- Life is short — enjoy it.

CHAPTER 12

POWER or PLAY:
How to take control

When you were attracted to someone, did you have butterflies in your stomach, stars in your eyes, wobbly knees? Perhaps, you were so attracted to that particular person that you felt quite powerless over yourself and your emotions.

If you were fortunate enough to have your feelings reciprocated, you will have experienced a different sense of 'powerlessness'. For many of us, the feeling of 'being in love' is wonderful. While it may only be infatuation, there is still a great sense of being out of control which can lead us into all types of playful behaviour.

When you are 'in love' or infatuated by someone, you dis-

cover you want to play the game of life and you quite innocently
begin playing games without realising that there might be a
power struggle going on. In many relationships, games are
played. Initially, the intentions may be good, but depending on
which direction the relationship goes, games can lead to destructive situations.

Let's take, for example, the fictitious case of John and Mary.
Mary really fancies John and while John was interested at the
start, he has now decided that he doesn't want to be involved.
Mary thinks about nothing else but John. Every minute of every
day is spent plotting how she will spend some time with him.
Even when John gently tells her he doesn't want to be involved,
she is so convinced by her fantasy relationship that it takes over
her life.

OBSESSIVE RELATIONSHIPS

Very often, the following scenario exists in so-called obsessive
relationships:

(1) Your partner is a crutch for you and you'd consider your
life worthless without him or her.

(2) You start to think solely of *your* needs, disregarding the
needs of the other person. A person in love wants what is best
for their loved one; a person obsessed wants what he or she
thinks is best for themselves.

(3) The person is constantly on your mind — you can't think
clearly or do normal day-to-day things.

(4) Other relationships — family, friends and work colleagues
— start to suffer. They don't seem to matter anymore. The only
person that matters is the person you consider yourself in love
with.

(5) You don't enjoy doing anything without that person,
including things you used to enjoy doing by yourself or in the
company of friends. Every evening is a total flop if you can't be
with that person.

(6) You refuse to face up to reality. The relationship might be

totally different in real life than it is in your fantasy, but you ignore this.

(7) You put the object of your obsession on a pedestal. You refuse to believe anything that paints a less-than-rosy picture.

(8) Obsessional love includes following the person around, or finding out things about them that they are not ready to divulge and then trying to use the information directly or indirectly to keep the person tied to you.

(9) You can't leave the person alone. You think nothing of phoning him or her ten times a day or calling around to see them out of the blue for no particular reason, regardless of how that person feels.

(10) You can't ever imagine life without the person. An obsessed person can do desperate things. You'd hurt that person rather than let him or her lead a life without you.

While obsessive relationships can be destructive, most of us get over infatuation and move on from playful romantic settings to more serious situations. In a relationship, playful behaviour is healthy provided it doesn't lead to manipulation.

However, alongside such games, there can be power struggles — deliberate or otherwise. Let's take another fictitious example. Patrick and Ann have been dating for some time and they decide to get married. Soon after they are married, Ann gets promoted in her job. She is now earning a higher salary than Patrick and would appear more qualified. While they had a good partnership, Patrick now feels threatened by Ann's new sense of power.

He perceives Ann's new status as giving her power in all situations and he finds himself becoming more vulnerable in the relationship. Even though Ann still feels the same about Patrick, his sense of being threatened could affect what had been a very stable relationship. Unless he can discuss how he feels with her, their relationship could crumble.

PERCEPTION OF POWER

How power is perceived is the essence of this issue. In other words, Patrick's perception of Ann's new-found status makes him feel powerless and gives Ann power over him. If he chooses to see Ann's new job differently (for example, that it gave her new strengths which could enhance their relationship), power might not have become the issue it was for him.

Power struggles can also occur at work. Sometimes you can feel intimidated by a particular person in your workplace and while that individual is anxious to help you with your job, your perception of their status makes you feel powerless and therefore unable to perform at your best.

In other work situations, some people are aware of having power and can use it to manipulate situations to get others to play along with their internal rules. What happens then is that power games are played. Sometimes, two people vie for the same position and they both play the game of being 'yes' people, constantly trying to please their boss.

In large organisations, there can be enormous competition for promotion and most people perceive promotion as power. The struggle for this power brings with it endless games of pursuing the boss, meeting the right people, saying the right things, while often losing sight of the actual job itself.

POLITICS IN THE WORKPLACE

In work situations, all sorts of 'politicking' can go on. People play such roles as the 'slick operator', the 'I can do everything' worker, the 'office telltale' who highlights other people's mistakes, or the 'regimental sneak' who sticks to the rulebook only when it suits them. Another familiar scenario is putting your personal life on hold, thinking that all work and no play will lead you to the top of the corporate ladder.

While most people don't set out to play these 'games', they can get caught up in what is going on around them, often to such an extent that they can cause themselves great stress which affects their performance at work. An enormous amount of time is wasted in politicking, game-playing and one-up-manship in order to achieve power.

However, the people who do finally achieve the power realise that it is not just about having 'one over on someone'; it can also bring with it huge responsibilities and strains. Nowadays, some people are choosing not to get involved in the games people play to get promotion. Steering clear of the corporate model of success, they are developing other ways of working where personal fulfillment is gained in a less competitive and manipulative way.

Power means you have influence over others and unless you have a clear knowledge of what that means and what responsibilities it brings, the power can have detrimental effects. If you seek power, ask yourself what it is you really want. Is it the status? The sense of superiority? The influence you will hold over people? Ask yourself is it what you really want because with every more senior position comes further demands and responsibilities along with the higher status and remuneration.

It must be remembered also that sometimes people who appear to have power in their workplace can be disempowered in other areas of their lives. Although they have managed to climb the corporate ladder and they appear to have succeeded in their working life, they can be very fragile in their personal lives. Sometimes it is almost like they have two personalities. Exercising excessive power in one's working life can sometimes be a compensation for a lack of control, fun or flair in one's personal life.

What we really need is balance — a mix of security and power in both our personal and working lives.

THE WAY FORWARD

- Give up playing manipulative games with yourself and others.

- Become aware of the power you have in your work and personal life.

- Don't abuse your power to the detriment of others.

- Remember that power can also bring responsibility and influence.

CHAPTER 13

VISIBLE versus INVISIBLE PAIN:
Integrating the mind and the body

Have you ever celebrated an event whereby you woke up the next morning feeling so good that you wanted to hold onto the feeling. You wish you could find a button that could make the world stand still so that you would never have to change your mood or feelings.

Different situations in our lives allow us to experience and enjoy these precious times — a birthday party, a first love, winning an important match, getting an exam, a new job, our wedding day, the birth of a child. Each event gives different pleasures to different people.

Such a sense of achievement and celebration leaves you with

an overwhelming sense of security, support and self-worth. You wish every day could be like this. Unfortunately, life isn't this way and with time, things change — both for the better and the worse.

For many of us, the bad days are associated with external pain — the tummy ache (before you went to school), the headache (before the first exam), the ulcer (before the major interview), the backache (after losing your job) or the heart attack (when you failed to get promotion).

HIDDEN PAIN

During these bad times, you go to your local doctor to sort out the problem. For example, if it is migraine you want the pain taken away instantly. You tell the doctor all your symptoms — the severity of your pain, exactly when it comes on, how long it lasts and how you are worn out with it. After five minutes talking about your ailment, your doctor gives you a pill to soothe your pain. For a day or two your pain eases, but gradually it creeps back because what you didn't tell your doctor was that your life was falling apart, or that your relationship was finished, or that you didn't get the promotion you were hoping for, or that your mortgage has just gone up, or that you had just crashed the car.

In a strange way, when you went to your doctor to tell him or her about your 'migraine', you half-hoped your other issues would be understood as well, even though they were never mentioned. These other issues are most likely the real cause of your migraine, but they are too painful to talk about because they make you feel less that a whole person. It is more acceptable to talk about the physical pain.

When you talk about your headache or your ulcer, you immediately evoke sympathy from others. In fact, you probably have plenty of listening ears. Perhaps other people empathise, sharing their stories with you, comparing notes. You suddenly belong to a group and are no longer so isolated. Your inner pain is eased for a while.

Medication can give instant relief and, appropriately used, alleviates pain. But where there is hidden pain — in other words, pain attacking your emotional system — tremendous courage is required to deal with it.

INNER TURMOIL

We live in a society that doesn't encourage us to speak about inner turmoil. It is much easier to mention physical ailments. It is not, as yet, acceptable to talk about the pain of heartbreak, the pain of losing a job, the pain of a relationship breaking up, the pain of not getting promoted, the pain of failing an interview. Neither is it acceptable to talk about the pain of humiliation, shame, guilt and abuse.

While we are moving more towards understanding psychological problems, we are still a long way from accepting people who can openly and courageously say, 'I have benefited from counselling or therapy'. Some people even feel ashamed for having gone because by doing so, they think they have exposed a weakness in themselves, which is even more painful.

Invisible pain is not tangible. It is not seen, but it is felt. Some of us don't give ourselves permission to talk about it, perhaps because we have no one to talk to. People think they are helping by giving us the standard answers — 'Sure, you will get over him, aren't you better off without him' or 'There will always be another job' or 'It wasn't the right time anyway'.

UNDERSTANDING

When we are going through the pain and agony of internal suffering, we don't want to hear such clichés. We don't want standard answers. We want someone to understand what we are feeling. We want someone to listen to what is actually going on. We want someone to touch us in the way a caring person may touch your forehead to soothe away a headache. But how can someone soothe away the inner pain? In some way, for people even to know about it, we have to open our hearts and talk about how we really feel. Unless somebody knows, they cannot understand. Unless somebody hears, they cannot know. Unless somebody is given the chance to listen, they cannot heal your wound.

Many factors contribute to us not wanting to share our internal pain. For example, childhood experiences linger in our minds, like being told 'Little boys don't cry', 'You must be brave', 'You must not let the side down'. Also when you cry in public or when you share your pain with somebody, you are asking the other person to deal with that pain. Perhaps, they don't know how and it is doubly painful to have shared your pain with someone who doesn't know how to cope with it. You may even end up comforting *their* inadequacy.

So often it is easier to bury your pain and not talk about it, pretending everything is alright, wearing the mask, putting up the barrier and playing the game of being able to cope when, in fact, you are falling apart.

BEING APPROPRIATE

In a way, we have to learn to be appropriate. It would not be a good idea to walk into your boss at an inappropriate moment and pour your heart out to him or her. We have to learn to seek the right person out at the right time. We must feel the person is giving us permission to talk and is hearing us — hearing not just our pain but also things that may not have been said.

Different cultures deal with hidden pain in different ways and we have to adapt to our specific culture. Many of us may not have the right person to share our pain with and so we seek the help of a professional who can be objective about our situation.

THE WAY FORWARD

- Recognise and acknowledge inner pain.
- Articulate your pain and get support.
- Be prepared to make some changes in your life.
- Try to learn from your experiences, both good and bad.

CHAPTER 14

TEA or THERAPY:

Support — professional, family or friends

'Would you like a cup of tea?' Very often when you ask some-body this, what you really mean is, 'Do you have some time to sit down and have a chat about some problems I'm having?'

There are times in our lives when the tears have dried up and we need to sit down over a cup of tea and spill our hearts out. When we are going through any crisis, there is no doubt that we need to share it and open our hearts to another human being. Often, we can find it difficult to talk to those closest to us, so we seek out a friend. Sometimes this works, sometimes it doesn't. If the friend has a lot of issues going on in his or her life, they may not be able to give you the support you really need. They may give you some time, but you still have the sense of needing to turn to someone else.

This is where professional counsellors and therapists come in, although for some reason we all have a sense of anxiety about going to them. Perhaps it is because our culture isn't ready for this yet or maybe it is because we have seen therapy used badly on television or in movies.

Therapy or counselling, when used well professionally, can give you an enormous sense of support and insight into what is really going on for you in your life. Remember when you go to a therapist or a counsellor, you are just like a consumer and you have certain rights — you can demand.

YOU, THE CLIENT

As a consumer, you need to look to the following five areas: confidentiality, care, clarity, competence and cost.

Confidentiality — first of all, if for any reason you feel ill at ease, check out the 'confidentiality' aspect of your therapist: simply state that it is vital for you that nobody knows about what you discuss with them and then judge the reaction.

Care — this is something that you will sense when you meet the person. The therapist or counsellor must be a caring individual who respects your integrity and dignity, and can empathise with you. If for any reason you feel you will not be comfortable with the person you have chosen, you can decide to go to someone else.

Clarity — if you go along to a therapist without knowing anything about their particular approach, you have a right to ask about their method and the therapeutic goals they will set with you.

Competence — if you don't know the therapist, phone the society or association that the therapist may belong to, whether it be social worker, psychologist, psychotherapist, psycho-analyst, etc. Check out that the individual is a registered, accredited member of that specific organisation.

Cost — always check out the cost of each session and for how long the therapist would anticipate you should attend before starting therapy.

Therapy can be oriented towards the individual, group, family or couple. Don't feel inhibited in any way about checking your facts before you start because if the therapy is to work, you must feel confident about all the above aspects. You must feel happy about the professional relationship and feel free to ask anything you are unsure of before you embark on therapy.

In therapy, it is important that you feel supported, that you trust the person and feel that they are going to be effective. Finally, when you feel happy with the therapist, your sessions should flow easily. Always feel free to ask questions if you are unhappy with anything. After all, it is your life and if you value yourself, you should value the time and energy you are putting into this. Therapy or counselling done well can give you enormous insight into yourself and improve the quality of your life.

If, for any reason, you cannot afford therapy, you could consider getting support from a trusted friend. You could negotiate with this person in such a way that he or she would listen in a non-judgmental way and give you support at a time when you need it. It is important that you negotiate this and not do it in a haphazard fashion. You should simply ask the friend if he or she would be free for an hour or two. And if the person needs you that you will also be available for them.

The problem is that if you don't structure your support sessions in this way, then when you ring your friend, you may start off talking about something quite different to what you really want to talk about. Alternatively, you may end up listening to their problems and never get to say what you intended. Therefore it is better to plan a time and make a point of saying that there is something specific you want to talk about.

Even for the approach of 'a chat over a cup of tea' to work effectively, time, energy and attention are necessary and also for you to be prepared to be truthful, effective, open and responsive to support.

SELF-HELP GROUPS

Nowadays, there are numerous self-help groups available to suit various situations. Generally, each support group has a basic philosophy which people adhere to; for example, Alcoholics Anonymous (also known as AA) is based on a 12-step programme which all members are encouraged to follow.

All self-help groups have in common the notion of mutual support: everyone in the group has the same problem (be it drink, overeating, depression, etc) and recovery is based on adhering to a fixed programme and giving mutual support to one another. For further information, please see the Appendix on page 80.

DIFFERENT TYPES OF THERAPY

Let's look at the different approaches of therapy. Firstly, it is important to distinguish psychotherapy from psychiatric treatment, which is generally prescribed by medically qualified doctors in psychiatric hospitals or in private clinics. In Ireland, psychotherapy is divided into five main branches — psychoanalysis, family and marital therapy, cognitive-behavioural therapy, humanistic therapy and constructivist therapy.

Psychoanalysis — the goal of this therapy is to make the unconscious conscious. This is done through dream analysis and free association of thoughts while the patient lies on a couch or otherwise relaxes. It is a prolonged form of therapy which can take several years to complete. The restructuring of the personality is more the aim than the solving of immediate problems.

Family and marital therapy — this form of therapy focuses on the personal dynamics between the couple and/or the members of the family. It concentrates on bringing to the surface conflicts between the individuals and finding ways of resolving issues that create disharmony.

Cognitive-behavioural therapy — this focuses on the explicit behaviour of the individual and his or her thinking processes. The aim of the therapy is to correct inappropriate ways of thinking and therefore to allow the client to behave in new, more personally adaptive ways.

Humanistic therapy — this focuses on the present interpretation of problematic events from the past. The client learns to understand better how and why he or she has reached a certain impasse in their life and how to move forward from it.

Constructivist therapy — this focuses on the different aspects of each individual personality and how they can come into conflict with each other and with other individuals. Its aim is to help the client understand how to integrate different personality characteristics better and thus how to lead his or her life in a more aware and controlled manner.

THE WAY FORWARD

- When life seems difficult, don't hold back — initiate support for yourself.

- If situations are really difficult, seek out a professional counsellor or therapist. Remember therapy is money well spent.

- Choose the therapy and therapist that suits you.

- Value yourself and your therapy sessions.

CHAPTER 15

OVER TO YOU:

Your choice — where to from here

Having got this far, you are now ready to move forward at every level and create the 'NEW YOU'. Like throwing out old junk, there is a right time for everything, and now is the time for you to discard all the old baggage that prevents you from being the person you really want to be. Go on, don't be afraid to do it!

You are now more aware and more enlightened about yourself and your own specific needs. You no longer have the excuse of not knowing how to move forward. You should have no more time for the 'poor me' syndrome, the 'I'm bored' feeling, the old cop-outs like 'I'm stuck in a rut' or 'I was given a bad deal'. Life is about grabbing opportunities, so now is YOUR chance.

Perhaps you'd like to write down all the changes that you have decided to make en route — changes relating to your thinking, your feelings and your behaviour. Use the 'Notes' pages at the back of this book. Write down the changes to be made in any order you want. For example, you may find that you want to see results fast so therefore your behaviour is the first thing you are going to concentrate on.

Indeed, when you change your behaviour, you usually feel better. You know yourself what it is you want to change, where it is you want to be and how you are going to achieve this. Don't make excuses or let anyone stand in your way. For every change that you make from the old to the new, give yourself a small reward — a bunch of flowers, some chocolates, a magazine, a tape, a new outfit, a book, a fun item like a teddy bear, or simply give yourself a big hug. This is your way of saying to yourself 'Well Done!'

While some of you may think this is a very selfish way of living, those around you will benefit from your more positive outlook on life. Remember, you don't have to feel alone. You can even start up your own support network for creating new ideas and implementing them.

Start your own book for new projects that you can constantly update and renew as you move on and make other changes in your life. Above all, enjoy what you do and don't apologise to anyone for this enjoyment. You've come this far, give yourself a well-deserved clap on the back. Go forwards knowing that no matter what life brings your way, you can never really go backwards from here.

THE WAY FORWARD

- Well done! You've got here at last.
- Live your dreams, not someone else's.
- Be proud of the 'new you'.
- Be positive and enjoy everything in life.

GOOD LUCK

and now

BLOOM!

APPENDIX

KEY INFORMATION SERVICES

Health Promotion Unit
DEPARTMENT OF HEALTH
Hawkins Street, Dublin 2
Tel: 6714711

Directory of National Voluntary Organisations,
Social Service Agencies and other useful public bodies
NATIONAL SOCIAL SERVICE BOARD
71 Lower Leeson Street, Dublin 2
Tel: 6616422

Alliance for Mental Health: Reference Manual
THE MENTAL HEALTH ASSOCIATION OF IRELAND
Mensana House, 6 Adelaide Street,
Dun Laoghaire, Co. Dublin
Tel: 2841166

THE WAY FORWARD
Notes

NOTES

NOTES

NOTES